Writing Exercises

for

Writers' Groups

(Including How To Start A New Writers' Group)

A Handbook For Workshop Facilitators

Joan C. Harthan, PhD

ISBN: 9798825534428

Contents

Acknowledgements

I would like to thank my copy editor and beta reader, Tony Casson, for helping to sort out the challenge caused by the lack of singular, gender-neutral pronouns in the English language.

Thanks must also go to the many writers and writers' groups for generating within me the ideas that were the basis of the writing exercises in his book.

INTRODUCTION

This book is a collection of more than one hundred writing exercises, each one designed to be completed within fifteen minutes. They are presented here as exercises for writing groups but can just as easily be done by individuals working alone. They provide a fun way to stimulate creativity and release writers from that dreaded strait jacket of writers' block.

A Word About Writing Groups

Writing is generally a lonely pursuit even though most writers are only too happy to have long periods when they shut themselves away from the world. It is true that the 2020/2021 covid lockdown was a blessing for some of us; a chance to complete all those outstanding projects. However, you can have too much of a good thing and it's not unusual for writers to sometimes feel isolated and alone — especially when family and friends would prefer you to be out socialising with them instead of trying to finish your latest project. But don't despair; there is solace and support to be found in writers' groups.

Writing groups provide you with a tribe of like-minded people. People who understand what you're trying to achieve and, more importantly, are interested and committed in helping you succeed. Most groups are an eclectic mix of professionals, semi-professionals and amateurs. You will find novelists, poets, short story writers, playwrights and a whole mixed bag of genres. Everyone, no matter how inexperienced, has something to offer the group and there is always something new to learn. Apart from providing valuable feedback, writing groups are an excellent forum for the exchange of ideas about the craft of writing.

Even during the covid pandemic, many writing groups continued to meet online. I know technology can be a thorn in our side sometimes but it proved its worth during those long months of isolation.

So, if you're not currently a member of a writers' group, I strongly suggest you join one. If there aren't any groups in your area, the second part of this book will help you to start your own group. I promise you, the rewards will be worth the effort.

PART ONE

15 minute Creative Writing Exercises

CHAPTER 1
Why Fifteen Minutes?

Fifteen minutes works well because what is produced in that time is short enough for all members to share their completed exercise with the rest of the group by reading it out loud. Most people will write between 200-300 words. When working alone at home or with very small groups you may wish to give a longer time. The aim is to energise and stimulate the creative juices, not to produce a finished work.

When undertaking an exercise, it's important to just let the words flow unimpeded. Sometimes the words or phrases you would normally have deleted are like diamonds in dust or can become the seeds of a new project.

You should write quickly without thinking too much about it and definitely without editing. Some people find this difficult initially and there will no doubt be complaints from some members of the writing group if the exercise chosen requires them to write outside of their usual genre. If this happens, convince the procrastinators to try it without judgement. Be confident that by the end of the exercise even they will be amazed at what is produced in so short a time. The finished piece can quite often be modified later and included in a current project giving an unexpected twist or turn of events. To use an old cliché, the proof is in the pudding and you can be sure that any complainers will soon be silenced.

Save, Save, Save

Nothing in a writer's portfolio should ever be wasted so I encourage you to save every completed exercise.

Every fifteen minute exercise I have ever done in writing groups is filed on my computer and every so often I go through the files and pull out things to develop further. These short pieces, with editing and revisions, lend themselves very well to a piece of flash fiction. I have mentioned a couple of websites that accept flash fiction submissions with no entry fee in the Resources section at the end of the book.

Many of the exercises will pull you out of your comfort zone and lead you in directions you may never have thought of going. This can be exhilarating. Quite often I will re-read the product of an exercise years later and find myself astounded at the ingenuity and unpredictability of the piece. It often feels like I'm reading the piece for the first time; almost as though it was written by someone else. Imagine the joy of that. It's a great confidence booster.

CHAPTER 2
A Writers' Toolbox.

Before we launch into the exercises, I would like to suggest that you spend a little time assembling a writers' toolbox in the form of prompt cards.

Prompt Cards

Prompt cards can take many forms and are easy to make. Cut stiff paper or card into rectangular pieces — 3cm x 6cm works well. Write (or type) a single prompt on each card. Aim for about twenty cards in each of the following categories. Suggestions as to content is given.

Occupation **prompts** — e.g. plumber. doctor. dentist. road sweeper. builder. journalist. police inspector. salesperson. window cleaner etc...

Person **prompts** — e.g. young girl. toddler. mother. sister. old man. teenager etc . . .

Genre **prompts** — science fiction. romance. historical fiction. crime. psychological thriller. comedy etc...

Objects **prompts** — e.g. red shoes. hammer. book. yellow raincoat. train. three-legged stool. old bookcase etc . . .

Emotion **prompts** — e.g. love. hatred. anger. ambivalence. friendship. rage etc...

These prompt cards can be used in many different ways. For example: have two categories available and place each in a pile face down or place them in separate envelopes or bags. Blindly take one card from each category. Swapping is not allowed! You then have fifteen minutes to work with what you have. Usually the most difficult combinations get the best results.

Other exercises using these prompt cards are included in the alphabetical list of exercises that follow.

CHAPTER 3
An Alphabet Of Writing Exercises

AD LIB

Without too much thought, write down four adjectives (descriptive words like green or soft). Now write down three nouns (things like desk, Edward). Follow that with two verbs (doing words like running, talking) and one adverb (these modify verbs such as 'she ran **quickly'**). Adverbs usually end in -ly though not always. The challenge is to write a short piece of prose using all those ten words.

ADVERT

You have decided to sell your very expensive binoculars. Write an advertisement extolling the usefulness of this item then write a few paragraphs explaining why you have to sell them.

AGE DEFINING

Write a 50-100 word character sketch for three of the following characters, giving a clear impression of their age without mentioning how old they are. Use only mannerisms, behaviours and physical appearance.

ninety year-old man
seventy five year-old woman
fifty five year-old man
thirty five year-old woman
twenty year old young man.
fourteen year old girl.

A KNIFE, A BOX, SOME TWINE AND LEG OF A PIG

A man walks into a supermarket and purchases a kitchen knife, a large storage box, some garden twine and a leg of pork. Loading it all into his truck, he drives away into the forest. What does he do there?

ANIMAL METAPHOR

Choose an animal, insect, mollusc or arachnid — in fact anything that moves and breathes and is not human. Make a quick list of all the characteristics of that animal. How does it move? Does it have a smell? What does it feed on? What colour and temperature is it? Where does it like to live? Engage all your senses.

Now transfer those animal traits to a fictional human character and place them into an imaginary setting where those character traits are apparent and are being expressed. Let the animal's voice flow through the writing.

A SUDDEN CHANGE OF PLAN

You have two minutes to come up with five scenarios of plans suddenly being changed. For example — travelling to the USA and the plane lands in Asia.

Once you've done that, choose one of the ideas to develop further and write at least a hundred words.

AUTOBIOGRAPHY

Take some inanimate object that features in your life at the moment and write a little autobiographical piece about it. How have you interacted with it? What have you done with it? What effect has it had on your life? Make sure your story is interesting and engaging. As an extra challenge, make it a comedy sketch.

A WALK IN THE WOODS

Take a photo of a dirt path running through a wood — a photo of a bluebell wood works really well. Imagine you are walking barefoot along the path and write either a piece of prose or a poem that describes your thoughts as you walk. Perhaps you are thinking of something in the past, or perhaps thinking about where you are going or who you will be meeting. Describe all the sensations of sight, smells, hearing and touch. Live and breathe the walk along the path through the wood.

This could be done as a real exercise — an excursion into the real world. Perhaps take a picnic and have a fun day out, (see Group Endeavours).

BIRD TALK

Choose one of the following birds: Blackbird. Canary. Crow. Dove. Eagle. Magpie. Owl. Pigeon. Raven. Robin. Seagull. Swallow. Now find your chosen bird in the list below and see what is the associated symbolism for that bird. Write a piece of flash fiction based around that theme. Mention the bird in passing at least once.

Blackbird - the healing power of nature.
Canary - the power of song and voice.
Crow - sensing danger.
Dove - forgiveness or divine inspiration.
Eagle - great power and clear vision.
Magpie - thief or bringer of good fortune?

Owl - inner wisdom.
Pigeon - returning home.
Raven - magic and mystery.
Robin - Joy and happiness.
Seagull - taking whatever one needs.
Swallow - flying high.

BORED AND TIRED

You are a student who only managed three hours sleep last night. Taking your place at the back of the lecture theatre, you are hoping to avoid the scrutiny of the eagle-eyed lecturer whose talk is very boring. You should be taking notes but instead you write a soliloquy of your thoughts for the upcoming university 'Spoken Word' evening.

CHANGING POV

For this exercise you will need a photograph or picture of at least three people who appear to be in conversation. Choose one of the characters and write a paragraph about the encounter from that POV. Then choose another of the characters and write a paragraph from a different POV.

CHILD NARRATOR

Remember an episode or an incident from your childhood. Recount the situation in the words of a child using first person, present tense. Use the simple language of childhood, thinking about how a child would view the situation. What analogies would the child be capable of making?

COULD YOU DO THIS?

Write a piece of free verse with the word 'Could' or any homophone (e.g. cud) in every line of the poem.

CREATE A NEW WORLD

You're standing at the boundary between two worlds. The world behind you is the one you are leaving behind. Why are you leaving? How do you feel about that? What does the new world look like? What are you expecting to find there?

DAY OF THE DEAD

It's raining and people are standing around a grave as a coffin is lowered down. You catch the eye of one of the other mourners. Who is it? Who are you? Who is in the coffin?

DEVELOPING A CHARACTER

This is a really useful exercise for those who already have a project underway and feel that one of the characters is too thin or maybe too stereotypical. The idea is to write a brief character sketch concentrating only on appearance, beliefs and mannerisms. As well as portraying an imaginary character, it's also a fun exercise to do based on someone you actually know — after all aren't most of our imagined characters the result of direct observation? Just remember that if you use a real person, give your character a completely different name; you don't want to be the subject of a libel action.

DOPPLEGANGER

Write a first person account of meeting someone who looks exactly like you. Who is this person? Where has he/she come from? Has this person sought you out or is this an accidental meeting? Do you notice any subtle differences in the doppleganger's appearance or mannerisms?

DRUNK IN CHARGE

Imagine you have had one too many beers and have decided to go shopping in your local supermarket. Write a first person POV of your drunken exploits pushing a trolley around the store looking for what you want to buy.

ENRICHING STEREOTYPES

It's easy to fall into the trap of using stereotypes in your work, especially for inexperienced writers. Stereotypes are flat characters who are predictable and boring for the reader. This exercise will help you think outside the box and add depth and interest to your characters.

This task uses the prompt cards mentioned in Chapter 2: A Writers' Toolbox'. Choose a card from the 'Occupation' or 'Person' pile. And write a couple of paragraphs for the stereotype you have chosen. Show the character engaging in some expected activity. Now write another scene which makes the character more complex by having the person behave or think in a way that goes against our expectations. For instance, a counsellor who never stops talking. The man who cheats on his wife but gets angry when his mistress lies to him. The Health & Safety Inspector who has loose wires and trip hazards all over his house.

EVOCATIVE DESCRIPTIONS

Take the following phrases and include them in a piece of writing. However, you must radically change the wording by beefing up the phrases to make your readers really feel they are in the scene you are describing. Add whatever you feel necessary but make sure you are showing and not telling. As for Roger, try and give an impression of his character; perhaps from his clothes and the way he is walking.

It was a crisp spring morning. *(e.g. frosted grass, not yet warmed by the spring sun, crunched beneath my feet).*
It had rained all day yesterday. *(e.g. yesterday the sky had been leaden and the grass sodden).*
The daffodils were wilted.
The newly mown lawn was very green
Roger was walking towards me

EXPLORING AN EXISTING CHARACTER

Choose one of the characters in your current project. Place the character in an unusual or difficult situation. Choose a scenario that is ridiculously challenging and show how the character copes with it.

The beauty of this exercise is that it encourages you to add depth to a character you are already working with, to make a more plausible human being. Quite often you will end up with a scene or situation that you can add to your current writing project to give the plot or storyline a bit of an unexpected twist. The aim is to understand how the most effective plots are driven by a character forging its own destiny.

FACING FEAR

Fear is a great component for causing conflict. Imagine a situation where someone is facing something frightening. The fear felt may be because of something physical (e.g. heights, dogs) or something within, (e.g. rejection, confrontation). Describe how the character reacts in this fearful situation. What does he/she do to overcome the fear?

FAVOURITE PLACE, WORST PLACE.

Spend a few minutes thinking of your favourite place. It might be somewhere outside, perhaps a wood or a beach, or an indoor place, perhaps a pub or cafe, or maybe your friend's house. You could even close your eyes and imagine the place in all its glory. Think about the colours and the smells. What's the weather like? Is anything moving? Who else is there? Jot down a few notes.

Now do the same with the worst place you can imagine. Somewhere you feel very uncomfortable or even fearful.

The exercise is to write approximately a hundred words about each place, capturing the feeling and the ambience. The writing should be descriptive and give a flavour of how you feel within each location.

FIRST AND THIRD PERSON

A first person account is a personal narrative with events seen directly through the main character's eyes. The narrator is inside the head of the character and is privy to that person's deepest thoughts and desires. E.g. 'I walked into the room. With relief, I saw that everything was set out as I'd requested.' First person narrative does, however, limit the amount of information available to the main character.

In third person, the narrator is not a character in the story but is able to see into the mind of the main character and is also able to see what happens to all the other characters. In this case, the narrator will see things that the main character doesn't see. E.g. 'Sharon entered the room, relieved to see that everything was in order. She didn't notice the waiter hiding under the table.'

The first task is to write a one hundred word, third person account of a character walking into a potentially difficult situation.

Now write exactly the same scene in a first person narrative.

This exercise will prompt a discussion about the difference in the two pieces and when each may be better employed over the other.

FIVE WORDS

Jot down five words or phrases off the top of your head under the following categories:

The first word should be a **location**.
The second a **colour**.
The third a **feeling**.
The fourth an **action**
The fifth an **object**.

Now write an enticing piece of flash fiction using all five words.

FORBIDDEN

Your character has been told not to do whatever it is he/she is doing. There will be a high price to pay if discovered doing this forbidden thing. What is the risk? Include in the piece not only actions but also the feelings and the fear of being discovered.

FUSED CHARACTER

Take four people who are known to you in real life. Write down what you see as the main character trait of each person. Now imagine all of those traits fused into one person — this will be your fictional character.

Write a scene where your fictional character is struggling with an inner conflict caused by these disparate traits.

GOING HOME

A runaway has decided to return home. Without money, there is no choice but to hitch a ride from strangers.

What is the character thinking as he/she stands at the side of the road, watching the passing cars, hoping for a lift? Does a car stop? If so, who is it that is offering a lift?

GENDER SWITCH

This exercise plays around with male and female voices. Beware, it may well highlight your own gender bias and beliefs about the difference in the sexes. It may also stimulate interesting discussions, especially in mixed groups, about whether males can authentically write in the voice of a female protagonist and vice versa.

Imagine a character of the same gender as yourself and put him or her into a situation of conflict or difficulty. Perhaps he/she witnesses a theft or a violent confrontation, or maybe encounters prejudice or some sort of obstacle.

Next, take exactly the same situation but now your character is of the opposite sex. How does the dialogue / action change?

HERO'S JOURNEY

Almost all successful books and movies are an adaptation of the archetypal hero's journey. It's a popular format because it speaks to the higher psychological values of all human beings. We all fundamentally want to transcend our difficulties and become a hero/heroine in our own lives.

This exercise is more in-depth than the others and can be used as an on-going project over a number of weeks to initiate and develop a character. It's also a very interesting exercise to use on yourself — if you dare. You go down the rabbit hole as far as you wish to go.

The first step is to write just one or two sentences for each of the twelve stages. You can either do this for an imaginary character OR apply it to yourself and your own life, adding a bit of literary licence if necessary. To use it as an on-going exercise, each step would be fleshed out and developed week by week. The twelve stages are as follows:

1. Ordinary Life. (What does the character do for a job? Family? Friends? Preoccupations?)

2. The Call to Adventure. (Whatever it is must be something that seems almost unattainable).

3. Refusal of the Call. (Can't do it. Too afraid. Not skilled enough. Outside pressure to refuse).

4. Meeting the Mentor. (Someone or something that tells the hero, yes you can do it).

5. Crossing the Threshold. (The decision to accept the adventure is made).

6. Tests/Allies/Enemies. (The true characteristics of the hero are revealed. He/she will discover unknown strengths. There will also be defeats and setbacks. It won't be easy but the hero will meet allies who will help).

7. Belly of the Whale. (The final separation from the hero's known world and self).

8. The supreme ordeal. (Life-or-death moment that is either physical or psychological. It is the biggest test but the hero has acquired skills during the journey that will ensure he overcomes this peril without compromise).

9. Reward or (metaphorically) seizing the sword. Victory.

10. The decision to go back to the 'old life' and take back the wisdom gained.

11. Resurrection. (One final test is required for the purification and rebirth of the hero. Alternatively, it may be a miraculous transformation; a new way of living in the old world. There has been a symbolic death and rebirth).

12. Return with the Elixir. (The triumphant hero returns to the ordinary world bearing treasure, love, freedom, wisdom, or knowledge).

HOW YOU SAY IT.

Imagine three very different characters who have found out a man is cheating on his wife. One is a close female friend of the wife, one is the brother of the cheating husband and the third is a nosy neighbour from the local shop.

Concentrating on dialogue and body language, how will each of the three characters tell the wife of their discovery — assuming that each is the first to tell her?

I FEEL REALLY UNCOMFORTABLE.

Think about an incident or a time when you felt really uncomfortable. Think about how you felt and what you did to try and alleviate the discomfort.

Now either write about the real incident in a fictitious setting OR think about something novel or unpredictable that you could have done (but didn't) to rid yourself of the discomfort /embarrassment.

INVENTING A NEW CHARACTER

We all make subconscious connections when we hear a name for the first time. Some names sound strong, some weak, some clever, some posh . . . you get the idea. In this exercise you will write down the first name of your grandmother and give the character the surname of the last thing you ate. That's where the name Polly Nitbit came from in the 'Opening Sentences' exercise. Or you could use the name of your favourite pet added to the maiden name of your grandmother Most of you will have seen these going round Facebook. It's a fabulous, fun way to conjure up unusual characters that could well end up in one of your projects.

The exercise is to write a character sketch of the name you have conjured up. To make it more interesting, and slightly more challenging, why not conjure up two names using each of the methods mentioned and put the characters together in an unusual encounter.

IT'S ALL ABOUT FOOD

Write a short piece about some particular food. Whether observing, buying, eating or cooking it. Whatever it is, there must be a consequence — a price to pay, good or bad. It can either be real or imaginary food.

JEKYLL AND HYDE

Write one hundred words centred around a heroic character. Put him/her into a situation where the heroism is actively shown.

Next write another one hundred words about the same character but this time put the character into a completely different situation that causes a transformation into an anti-hero or antagonist.

JUST ANOTHER DAY

The protagonist of your story has popped out on a mundane errand — perhaps he/she has gone to buy milk from a local shop. Write about this errand in an interesting and engaging way, relying solely on the character traits of the protagonist.

KILLER OPENING LINES

This exercise uses the prompt cards mentioned in Chapter 2: A Writers' Toolbox. Have people randomly choose just one card from the 'Objects' pile and then write some killer opening lines, all of which include the item on the card that's been picked. The lines should be intriguing and also written to hook the reader in.

The next step is to choose one of the opening lines and expand it for 10-15 minutes using as much sensory detail as possible. Include a mystery and a cliff hanger at the end.

KILLING A CHARACTER
Describe, graphically but without melodrama, a fight between two characters resulting in the death of one of them. Drop into the narrative **subtle hints** about their different characters and why they are fighting.

LETTER OF INVITATION
Write a letter inviting someone to a party. Mention who else has been invited and the fun things that have been planned.

Write another letter as the responder to the invitation, making it clear why you will not be attending.

LETTER OF TERMINATION
Imagine a dystopian world where the government is autocratic and un-elected. Write an official letter sent by a government department to a civilian terminating an agreement / contract / payment etc . . . Give a flavour of the dystopian world in your letter.

LOOKING THROUGH A MIRROR
Imagine you're in a room where there is a mirror that truthfully reflects everything that appears before it. You think you know yourself pretty well, yet when you stand in

front of the mirror you can't help noticing there is something very strange about your reflection. Perhaps it's distorted, or maybe there's something attached to you that is normally invisible. Or perhaps something else entirely. Describe what you see and what conclusion you come to about it?

LUCKY DIP

	Character	Trait	Weather	Location	Object
1	Grandmother	Daring	Drought	Theatre	Poker
2	Butler	Painfully shy	Stormy	Mountain	Axe
3	Gardner	Talkative	Raining	Village pub	Wheelchair
4	Writer	Clever	Sunny	School	Red car
5	Policeman	Naive	Cloudy	Forest	Laptop
6	TV presenter	Subdued	Windy	Playground	Bicycle

The Table above is for illustration purposes. You can include anything you like under each category. Only the headings must remain the same.

Write a list of the words: Character. Character. Trait. Trait. Weather. Location. Object. On the right of this list, write seven random numbers from 1 to 6. For example:

Character   5
Character   6
Trait   4
Trait   1

Weather   3
Location   4
Object   2

With reference to the table on the previous page, assign the number allocated to what is written in the table. See the completed example below.

	Random number	Assignations according to the Table above
Character	5	Policeman
Character	6	TV presenter
Trait	4	Clever
Trait	1	Daring
Weather	3	Raining
Location	4	School
Object	2	Axe

Now write a piece of fiction using all the prompts that were randomly chosen.

MEANINGFUL DIALOGUE.

This is a great exercise in 'show don't tell'. For this method you will need pictures of two people. Be inventive in your search for illustrations — it may be a picture of a doctor and his patient, a married couple, family members or friends, work colleagues or teacher and pupil. The variety is endless.

The idea is to write dialogue between the two characters interacting in such a way that the character of each of the individuals is shown.

Avoid qualifying adverbs such as those words ending in 'ly', e.g. he answered quickly / angrily. Try and avoid 'he said' 'she said'. Instead use active words that add to the characterisation. Perhaps one of the people is getting angry with the other, rather than say:

"Definitely not!" said Mark. He was clearly becoming angry.

You could write something like:

"Definitely not!" Mark strode across the room, heading for the door, heavy boots pounding on the bare tiles.

MIX AND MATCH

For this exercise you will need a collection of pictures, either printed out or cut out of magazines. The pictures can be of anything; people or places, situations or events.

Randomly choose a picture and also a prompt card from the Genre category mentioned in Chapter 2: A Writers' Toolbox.

Write a short piece encapsulating both.

MORAL TALES

A moral tale shows how and why a character changes — the crux of engaging story telling. If the main character doesn't change and keeps on making the same mistakes, or engaging in the same sort of behaviour, the story is not very satisfying for the reader. Examples of a moral tale might be: 'a lesson learned', or 'success after failure' or maybe 'the worm turns'. There are many more.

Conjure up your own moral tale with a dynamic character at the heart. Plan out your story in the form of a pitch to an agent i.e. giving the nuts and bolts of the story and how it ends. Make sure your character starts out with a huge problem then decides what changes to make in order to overcome the obstacles and achieve the required outcome.

MYSTERY

A mystery should begin with a mystery. Spend a couple of minutes conjuring up a mysterious opening line for a crime novel.

Now think about the setting of your mystery — choose somewhere enclosed and having boundaries, like a house or a village. Next put a dead body somewhere shockingly out of place. You could also think about introducing a character who will provide a misdirection or red herring. Jot down your thoughts and ideas in note form.

From your notes, write a few enticing opening paragraphs for a mystery novel that will hook a reader.

NEWSPAPER HEADLINE

Keep your eyes open for interesting, evocative headlines in newspapers or magazines. Cut them out and start a collection of them. As an exercise, pick one out at random. Whatever the headline is, write a relevant news article.

To make it even more interesting, and slightly more difficult, pick two headlines and merge them into one headline and one story.

If you want more of a challenge, you could write a comedy sketch from the two amalgamated headlines.

NOBODY TOLD ME ...

Begin your piece with the words 'Nobody told me . . .' What weren't you told? Why is it important that you now know? Who else knows? Who kept it from you? How will your life change as a result of this news?

NONET

A nonet is something with nine components. In this case it is a nine line poem. It's an interesting and challenging exercise in writing poetry.

The idea is that the first line contains nine syllables. The next line has eight, the third line seven — right the way down to the ninth line which only has one syllable.

If guidance is needed, the first line could be some challenging situation in your current life, or maybe something as simple as a nature scene.

OPENING SENTENCES

This is a great exercise to illustrate how different we all are in our style of writing and the things we birth in our imagination. We are all unique — there will never be anyone else like us in the world again.

The idea is that everyone starts with the same opening sentence and each person writes a piece beginning with those same words. Some suggestions follow but sometimes I just choose a book from the library shelf and use that. Obviously if you do that you need to be aware that the quoted sentence will be subject to copyright laws. The beauty of this method is that it can also stimulate discussion about what makes a good opening line.

A few suggestions:

The day the magpie flew into the house was the day my world fell apart.

There's a wheelie bin on the pavement outside Number 32; it's been there for three weeks.

I dreamed about you last night.

Polly Nitbit lives next door, making pigeon pies to sell at market.

OUT OF CHARACTER

Randomly choose one of the 'Occupation' prompt cards outlined in Chapter 2: A Writers' Toolbox. Think about the qualities and attributes that person might have. Now write the character into a situation that goes against what he/she knows or believes to be right. For example: a doctor who knowingly prescribes harmful medication for an adversary, or maybe a policeman who doesn't book a friend for speeding.

Your story should deal with any potential guilt or recrimination.

POINTS OF DEPARTURE

To some extent our writing is derived from our own experiences. This exercise is about recovering points of departure from our own life and using one of them to write a fictional or autobiographical piece. Think about those times when you made a decision to leave something or someone behind.

Begin by drawing a circle in the centre of a piece of paper and writing in the centre of the circle 'Points of Departure'. Add spokes, like the spokes of a wheel. At the end of each spoke write what it was you left behind. It could be something as mundane as moving house or leaving a town to go on a camping trip, to something life-changing like divorce, or leaving school.

Once you've brain-stormed all your personal departure events, choose one to develop that still has an element of emotion. Now write down three column headings on the paper: Associative Memory / Narrative Memory / Associative Memory.

Under the middle column of Narrative Memory, write out the event step by step — one step under another and leaving a good amount of space between them. For instance, if you were departing a place, the steps might be: woke at 7am, packed suitcase, had breakfast, took bus to train station etc . . . Once you've done this start filling in Associative Memories on either side of each step. These are the memories of how you felt during that particular step. What part did others play?

There probably won't be time in fifteen minutes to go further than this but your notes can be developed further and will undoubtedly be useful for any number of new projects.

POLITICIAN SPEAK
Write a speech for a politician who believes, and wishes to convince others, that everyone (even the elderly) should abandon their cars and use electric scooters.

You may intersperse the speech with hecklers from the audience if you wish.

POSTCARDS
For this exercise you will need a collection of postcards. Wherever you go, be on the lookout for interesting and evocative ones that you can add to your collection. One of my favourites shows a pair of wellington boots disappearing into Glastonbury mud.

Once you have a collection, choose a card blindly — no picking or pandering to preferences. The exercise involves writing whatever comes to mind about the picture shown on the chosen postcard. You have free rein to use the picture in its entirety or to focus on just one aspect.

Another way, although one that requires a bit more intellectual thought, is to come up with a suitable metaphor or theme suggested by the picture and write a piece based on that. For instance the Glastonbury mud postcard may be 'sinking in mud' or 'going under' — both of which lend themselves to a more psychological theme.

PLOTTING VARIABLES

Your starting point for this exercise is a scene where a man walks into a cafe and sits down at a window table where a woman is already sitting.

Write the outline of this scene in four very different stories, changing the characters, the plot and the theme in each one.

QUADRUPLED

Four people, with very different personalities, witness a murder from completely different perspectives. They each have a different relationship to the victim.

One is the victim's partner, one is a friend of the perpetrator, the third is a complete stranger who just happened to be passing by, and the fourth is a blind busker who was sitting on the pavement playing guitar.

Write the witness statement of each character giving a unique voice to each.

QUARRELLING COUPLE

This exercise is designed to demonstrate how much can be conveyed using only body language.

Write from the POV of a stranger looking at two people engaged in a heated conversation. The stranger cannot hear the words spoken, only observe the couple's behaviour, appearance and actions.

The writing should include assumptions about the relationship between the two characters.

REFORMED CHARACTER

Your character has been in prison for a number of years and is about to be released. Something happened in prison that has resulted in a total reformation of character.

What was it that happened and how will it change the character's life on release?

REGRET

Think about a time in your life that you regret. This could be something that happened, a decision you made or a conversation you had. Try and choose something that still has strong emotion attached to it.

Re-write the incident with a different ending, one that would have had a completely different outcome.

SAME PATH, DIFFERENT MOOD

Imagine a path that leads through a field full of buttercups, primroses and clover. At the end of the field is a stile that leads into a wooded area where a babbling brook meanders through the trees. You can hear bird song and the soft rustle of leaves as the wind breezes through.

In approximately 100 words, describe your walk along this path on a day you have had some good news. You are happy and at peace with the world. Looking forward to the future.

The next task is to write about your walk along this same path on a day when you have had some bad news. You are out of sorts and moody. The future looks bleak and your energy is low. You feel utterly miserable and have no patience with anything.

The accounts should differ markedly, reflecting how you see the world in different states of mind. Try using the weather as an emotional metaphor to accentuate how you are feeling.

SETTING THE SCENE

Write max 100 words setting the scene for each of these genres:

1. A cosy crime e.g. Agatha Christie, Midsummer Murders

2. A Brit Grit noir (A dark tale with a British flavour)

3. Police procedural

4. How dunnit (NOT who dunnit).

SIBLING RIVALRY

Two sisters are in conversation. They are disagreeing about something important to both of them but they don't want a full-blown argument. Have them exchange their views by passive-aggressive snide comments.

SOMEONE'S KNOCKING ON THE DOOR

Why is someone knocking on the door in a manner that sounds impatient and angry. Who is it? What does this person want? Should the people inside the house open the door?

The task is to write a short sketch of this scenario as if it were a scene in a play, giving stage directions where appropriate. Include at least three characters.

SONG ON THE RADIO

Make sure your radio is tuned in to a music channel. Turn it on and listen to whatever song is playing at the time.

Now write a piece about something that the song brings to mind. It may be related to the song title, the song lyrics or a memory that the song stirs.

SPECULATIVE FICTION

Speculative fiction is a genre that is becoming ever more popular in the modern literary landscape. It is a chance to explore complex truths, bend genres and build worlds — all of which is of interest to many publishers, literary journals and readers.

The focus in this exercise is on daring sub-genre fiction, i.e. weird fiction, innovative science fiction and magical realism.

Chose one of the following as the topic and write a piece of flash fiction, maximum 200 words:

A baby has been born with four arms.

Meddling in the quantum world has catapulted the Earth into another dimension.

Fairies and gnomes are at war in my garden

STALKER

Write a first person account of being stalked along a dark street. Build the tension up to a climax. Who is it that is following you? Do you know the stalker? How do you feel? Fill your account with speculation and terror.

STRANGER THAN TRUTH

Imagine a highly improbable scene. Something that is very unlikely ever to happen. Bring the situation to life by dialogue and action only — without any description. Write in such a way as to make it totally believable.

If you're struggling to think of an improbable situation, use one of the following:

A friend turns up who you are sure died last year.

Someone who once tried to kill you, re-appears after ten years wanting to be your friend.

Your dog suddenly begins to talk.

You have somehow been teleported to a different country.

STREET SCENE

Take a photo of a street scene with people mingling. Try and choose a photo with at least six people.

Get inside the head of just one of the people in the photo and write a piece from that character's point of view. What is the person doing? thinking? feeling?

This exercise can be extended, or the photograph used over and over again, by writing from the POV of a different character each time.

STYLE IT OUT

Imagine you're at a social gathering when you spy an adversary across the room. You want to hide, make yourself scarce. You can't face this person because of what you (or your adversary) did BUT you decide to style it out. Be the stronger person. Be the Top Dog. Come out on top.

How will this meeting pan out?

SUNDAY MORNING COMING DOWN

For those of you who don't recognise this heading, it is the title of a song written by Kris Kristofferson. Sunday's are different to every other day — usually. Things happen on a Sunday that often don't happen on any other day. The words of the song are about a lonely man who is missing something he has lost.

What are your experiences or feelings about Sundays? Choose one experience or feeling and write about a character in the same situation.

TAROT GUIDANCE

You will need a pack of tarot cards for this exercise. Separate out all the cards that portray a person and put them face down in a pile. Make sure they are well shuffled. Put all the remaining cards in another pile. You will then randomly pick two cards from the pile with a human character and two cards from the other pile.

Use these cards to write a piece of prose depicting a situation involving the two characters within the setting of the other cards.

TEENAGE REBEL

A teenager has had enough of his/her parents disapproving of everything he/she does. There is a big family event coming up and the teenager has been warned to dress appropriately. Write the scene, with confrontational dialogue, of the teenager coming down stairs just as they are all about to leave for the event.

TEXT MESSAGING

Using first person POV write a transcript of the messages sent between two characters having an intense argument via texting.

Add to the characterisation by including your thoughts and mannerisms as you engage in the 'conversation'.

THE BOX

Picture a rectangular box in front of you. It's dimensions are approximately one foot long, six inches wide and three inches deep. Who does the box belong to? What sort of box is it? Is it locked or unlocked? Where is it kept? What's inside? Why is the box important? What is its story?

If more prompting is needed, begin the exercise with:

The box had been locked away in my grandmother's dresser since 1929.

THREE CARD PROMPT

This exercise uses the Prompt Cards outlined in Chapter 2: A Writers' Toolbox. Choose three cards from the 'Objects' pile and write a short piece including all of them.

THREE LITTLE WORDS

This exercise encourages you to write in poetry form but it works just as well as a piece of prose.

Write down a word that you find inspiring — it may be an activity, a feeling or something more abstract. Once done, write down another word that is associated with the first, and again to get a third word. The three words are then used in a three line poem to elucidate and expand on the feelings and ideas generated by the words.

This can be done in the form of a Haiku — a three line poem. The first line has five syllables, the middle line seven syllables and the last line five syllables. An interesting extension to this as a group endeavour is to have each participant cut up their haiku into the three separate lines. All the five syllable lines are placed in a pile together, and the same for the seven syllable lines. Each person then randomly picks two lines from the five syllable pile and one from the seven. The task is to re-assemble the random lines into a new haiku.

The ingenuity and apparent cohesion of what is produced is often truly amazing.

TRAFFIC JAM
Traffic is backed up for six miles on the motorway. All vehicles are stationary. Write accounts of the occupants of three vehicles — a Jaguar XJ, a Fiat Panda and a VW Beetle. Who are the occupants? What is their appearance and state of mind? What is the reason for their journey? How are they coping with the delay?

TRAIN SPOTTING
This is a similar exercise to Street Scene except in this case you will use a picture of the interior of a train carriage or of

people waiting on a railway platform. Such photographs can easily be found on the internet providing you don't infringe copyright. The photo should show at least two people, preferably more, who are either on a train or waiting to board. They are each going on a journey.

The exercise is to choose one of the characters shown in the picture and write from that person's POV.

What does the character have on its mind? Where is the character going and why? Is he/she happy/sad/indifferent or something else entirely?

TRITINA

A Tritina is a repetitive ten line poem using lexical repetition. The structure is three, three-line stanzas called Tercets and one single line to conclude. So ten lines in total. There is no rhyming pattern.

Choose three words that may or may not be related to each other. For instance: a) Fall b) Mist c) Icicles. The words don't have to be nouns; you can choose active verbs if you like. These three words will each end a line in the first tercet.

To explain the format, it is easier to give an example. Notice that the word at the end of each tercet, starts the next tercet. The final sentence contains all three words in the correct order. **(abc)**

I saw you yesterday and began to **fall (a)**
Thoughts clouded with **mist (b)**
Pierced my heart with **icicles.(c)**

Like daggers were those cruel **icicles (c)**
As I listened on the stairs for your foot**fall (a)**
Come back like a dream in blinding **mist (b)**.

There's rain inside that spiteful, weeping **mist (b)**
Stabbed with penetrating, punishing **icicles (c)**
Why do I keep embracing the **fall? (a)**

Today the **mist (a)** clears and the **icicles (b)** melt but I still remember the **fall (c).**

UNDER THE BED
You wake up in the middle of the night with a start and have a feeling that there is something or someone under your bed. Mustering all your courage you take a peek.

What do you find there and what are you going to do about it?

VISUALISATION
Visualise a character you know well from a book, film or TV. Try and get as much clarity as you can. Think about mannerisms, features and the way of talking. Once you have a clear image in your mind, begin to describe the person on paper without naming who it is. Perhaps place the character in a scene that demonstrates the traits or mannerisms they possess.

VOICE OF AN EVERYDAY OBJECT
Choose an everyday household object; one you are very familiar with. Spend a couple of minutes jotting down all its

functions and attributes. Once done, write a piece of prose or a poem in the voice of the object, i.e. become the object. Give it human emotions. How does it feel about the job it does? How does it feel about you?

WHERE'S THE ROAD GOING?

Imagine a thin, pale snake of a road slithering away into the distance, heading eastward. A man tells you it ends abruptly and goes nowhere but you know different. Describe your journey along the road. What awaits you at the end of it?

If you find visualisation difficult, you could use a picture of a road stretching away into the distance — though I do recommend that you practise visualisation first.

WHOSE ROOM IS THIS?

Imagine you have just walked into the bedroom of a child who is being fostered. You have never met the child and know nothing about it or its background.

Describe what you see in the room; include the thoughts/assumptions it prompts you to make about the child.

A variation of this exercise would be to take a picture of a room and write an account of the person who inhabits that room. This is rather like the TV programme 'Through the Keyhole' where contestants must guess who lives in the house by making inferences from what is seen.

WHY, WHY, WHY?

This is a great exercise for developing a character through a back story.

Two characters are in conversation. One character asks the other 'Why are you ...(put whatever you like here)'. The other character answers and this prompts another 'Why?' For example:

Why are you wearing red shoes? *Because I don't like blue ones.*
Why not? *Because they remind me of Edward.*
Why Edward? *He dyed all my shoes blue last year.*
Why did he do that? *He has issues and it seems I'd upset him.*
Why? What did you do? *I told him I was leaving him.*
Why? *Because he'd painted all the house blue, including the cat.*
Why blue? *It's his mother's favourite colour.*

WITNESS TO A ROBBERY.

You are waiting in a doctor's reception area. You have an appointment to see the doctor and he's running late. The receptionist has temporarily vacated her post. A man, sitting next to you, gets up from his seat, leans over the receptionist's desk, opens a drawer and removes a mobile phone. He then quickly exits.

What was this man doing thirty minutes earlier?

WORD SALAD

Take the list of words below and include them all in a piece of fiction. They can be included in any order. The most important thing is to write quickly without thinking too much about the story line.

Newspaper. Broken ankle. Yellow hat. Ginger tom cat. Table cloth. Wooden spoon. Itching.

Obviously you can vary this exercise by using a different set of words.

WORKING WITH A TITLE

This exercise uses the prompt cards outlined in Chapter 2: A Writers' Toolbox. Choose one card from 'Person' or 'Occupation' and one card from 'Objects'.

The first task is to write a mysterious, engaging title that includes both words, bearing in mind that titles are probably the most important and most powerful hook for a reader. Jot down as many titles as you can think of in two minutes.

Next ask; 'What would my character want? What would he/she do to get it?' How will that action propel the story towards a crisis and final resolution?

Make the situation as complicated as you like. The aim is to draw your readers in, compelling them to keep on reading.

WRITING GROUP DISPARITY

Imagine a fictitious writers' group. There are six members and each one has a unique idiosyncratic quality. One is totally eccentric, one dresses in a peculiar fashion, one only writes about hamsters, another has Turrets syndrome. One of them has a nervous tic and is constantly raising his arm and shouting 'up the workers' and the last member believes the president of the USA is a reptile.

The group has decided to enter a writing competition. The remit is to write a short novella as a joint venture. The competition rules state that the piece must be written in the style of the party game 'consequences', with a slight variation. The first person writes two or three lines, folds the paper over, leaving the last line exposed, and passes it on for the next person to write two or three lines. And so on around the group.

The first task for you is to assign a name to each member of the writing group.

Next, write a scene where the group is sitting around a table discussing what would be the best plot line for the novella. There are bound to be disagreements and conflict. Hopefully, there will also be a certain amount of comedy for the reader to enjoy.

X-RAY VISION

X-ray vision is a term that describes the ability to see through solid objects. Comic strip heroes such as Kryptonians, Daxamites and Martians are among those who possess this ability.

Imagine a super hero/heroine who possesses a variation of this skill and has the ability to see exactly what a person is thinking, despite what that person says to the contrary.

Conjure up a scene where your super hero's skill is demonstrated in a public forum and results in the bad guy being exposed. If you're having trouble conjuring up such a scenario, think party political broadcast — that should fire your imagination.

XYLOPHONE

As you walk down the street you pass a waste skip. On the top is a xylophone. It has a ticket attached to it with a piece of string.

The ticket reads *'To Jamie from an admirer'*.

Who is Jamie, why is he admired and where is he now?

YEARNING FOR CHANGE

Write about a character who is stuck in a bad situation and yearns for change although change seems impossible.

Explore the frustration and feelings of helplessness by using active descriptions of the character and their surroundings.

YELLOW IS THE COLOUR

Think about the colour yellow. What things are yellow? Flowers? Paint? Sun? How does the colour yellow make you feel? Happy? Buoyant? Now jot down any further associations that spring to mind.

The task is to write a poem about yellow without using the word 'yellow'.

This exercise can be extended or altered by substituting with any colour.

ZOMBIE IN MY HOUSE

You wake up one day to find your son or daughter acting in a strange manner. Is he/she ill? Hung-over? Has something happened to cause upset? It transpires, during the course of the morning, that your offspring has turned into a zombie.

Write an account of your observations and the incidents that have led you to believe your child is now zombified.

ZOOM ZOOM

Write about an imagined incident occurring during an online Zoom meeting of a writers' group. If you wish, and to make it more realistic, you could have this take place during the covid lockdown.

How many people are taking part in the Zoom meeting? Who are the main players in the incident/conflict? Is the technology behaving itself?

Give a flavour of the personalities of the main players and describe how their different characteristics and aims resulted in the conflict or incident.

CHAPTER 4
Group Endeavours

Why not embark on a project or outing with your writers' group? There are many things you can do in this respect and here are just a few suggestions.

Of course, you can try out the group venture referred to in the Writing Group Disparity exercise above — if you dare.

ANTHOLOGY

An excellent project is to compile and publish an anthology. Seeing their work in print will give previously unpublished members of the group a great sense of achievement and something tangible to show their friends and family.

Clearly, if this project is undertaken you must ensure that the finished work is edited and formatted to the standard required for publication. You could use a professional editing service though this can be rather expensive. It is usually enough for two experienced members of the group to edit all the pieces and format the manuscript before submission.

Publishing can be done without any cost by using the Amazon kdp platform. Amazon also have the free Cover Creator software that allows you to design a professional looking cover. And, of course, author copies can be bought at a hugely discounted price.

If no one in the group has ever self-published, this will be a fabulous, hands-on learning experience for everyone and could well encourage some members to go down the immensely rewarding, independent route.

DAYS OUT

Wherever you live, there will be many places that are of interest to writers. This could be a visit to the birthplace of a famous writer or just a place of interest or beauty.

Why not organise a day out on public transport and give the group a specific task to be completed by the end of the day.

DYING TO WRITE

This involves a short meditation, which mostly everyone will find wonderfully relaxing. Make sure everyone is seated comfortably before explaining that they are going to go on an imaginary journey. Ask everyone to close their eyes and once everyone is settled, read out the following in a voice that is as soft and hypnotic as you can manage.

"Imagine you are a really hungry caterpillar. It's late summer and you are munching your way through big, juicy green leaves. Mmmm. . . they taste so good. You're getting fatter and fatter, and more and more tired. Your body is starting to feel heavy and bloated. It's a warm evening and the sun is setting. Every one of your hundred legs is starting to ache. You're so very tired. All you want to do now is sleep. So you cocoon yourself in a lovely, soft, warm duvet and are happy to just drift away into a dreamless sleep. Mmmm . . . that feels so good. Deep sleep. Dead to the world." (Pause)

"But then you wake up with no idea how long you have been asleep. You feel different. You're full of energy. And what's this? Where have all your legs gone? You've only got six left. And without knowing how you know, you recognise that you now have wings. You crawl out of your warm little bed, feeling excited at the prospect of exploring this new way of life. You emerge into a world that is exploding with bright, spring colours. Flowery scents fill the air. Bluebells and hyacinths. And vibrant green grass. There's cherry blossom and big, yellow dandelions. There has been a miraculous metamorphosis. You have been transformed into a butterfly. You can feel the hot sun on your back, drying your velvet wings. In a moment you will take to the air and fly away to start a brand new life . . . There you go. Carried away on a warm breeze."

Remain silent for a few seconds and then ask everyone to open their eyes and write down the first five words that spring into their mind from what they have just experienced. It's important that they don't think too much about this — encourage them to write down the first words that come to mind, even if they have nothing to do with the story.

Once done, make an announcement that certain words are not allowed. If anyone has written down caterpillar, butterfly, transformation or metamorphosis ask that those words are deleted from the list and other words written in their place.

Next, ask that everyone adds the word *blackbird* to their list.

The task is to take the six words and choose a theme related to death or dying and rebirth. It may be a poem or a piece of prose.

The death may be an actual physical death of a loved one or it may be more general feelings about death. It can also be the death of a behaviour or way of life.

EXHIBITION

Take good quality photographs of your local area and each week, during the fifteen minute exercise session, have everyone write a short piece of prose or poetry about the photograph for that week. If you can get a semi-professional photographer on board who is willing to enlarge the photographs for display, all the better.

You could then seek out a venue, maybe a library or museum, willing to exhibit your work as a community project. The idea is to have each photograph surrounded by the written pieces.

Providing there is no cost to hiring the venue this is an excellent way of cementing the group and attracting new members.

HALLOWEEN FUN

This is an excellent stimulus for digging deep into our vocabulary to come up with novel and interesting words and descriptions.

Ask the group to shout out all Halloween words that come to mind. Write down all the words on a whiteboard or flipchart so everyone can see them. When the words are exhausted ask everyone to write a short piece about Halloween WITHOUT USING any of the words that have already been written down.

This method can be used for any time of year, the seasons or festivities for example, or indeed applied to any topic or subject matter where the tendency is to regurgitate well-used words and phrases.

OBSERVING LANDSCAPE

Organise a picnic on top of a hill or in the centre of a town — actually anywhere would work well. The task for the outing will be to write about the surrounding landscape. Important aspects of landscape that could be dropped into the writing, include:

physical features
sounds and smells
touch / feel including wind and weather
economy / industry
taste
history
wildlife
human behaviour
dialect / language
clothing
food / diet
signage
light / weather
folklore / superstition
religion / religious buildings.
energy of place

The first exercise could be a piece of prose or a poem describing how each participant feels in that landscape.

The next may be a piece describing the actual landscape and what's going on inside it.

The third could be a piece of pure fiction, using the landscape as the setting.

ROLE PLAYING A DRAMA

Everyone randomly chooses one of the 'Person' prompt cards outlined in Chapter 2: A Writers' Toolbox. Each person will then spend a few minutes 'getting into character' — think about both physical and mental attributes. The idea is to immerse oneself completely into the character.

When all are ready, set the scene of the drama by explaining that the group is on an Atlantic cruise from Southampton to New York. After three days at sea, the body of a man is found at the bottom of the swimming pool. The ship's doctor estimates that he has only been dead about an hour. The victim has a tourniquet around his neck. He has been murdered.

Have slips of paper prepared — all blank except one that has the word 'murderer' on it and one that has 'detective' written on it. Each person picks blindly from the pile. Except for the detective, everyone must keep a 'poker face' so as not to give anything away to the others. Only the murderer knows his/her identity. This person must secretly devise a plan as to how and why he/she murdered the victim.

Have everyone assemble in a circle and advise them that one of them is the murderer. The detective begins by going round the circle inviting personal introductions, each in the guise of assigned characters. The detective can ask questions about the person's relationship to the victim and their movements in the last two hours. Once done, the other players can join in with questions. To make it even more interesting, one or two of the innocent characters could introduce some plausible 'red herrings'. When all questions are exhausted, suggestions as to who is the murderer can be thrown into the mix. It's only after this that the murderer reveals him/herself.

Follow the exercise with a discussion about how this scenario, with all these characters, might become a stage play. Appointing a director and acting out the story is sure to result in great hilarity.

WALK IN NATURE

Find a quiet place nearby and have everyone meet there on the day of the scheduled meeting. The exercise is to glean as much sensory information as possible and write a piece of free verse about the experience.

Encourage people to remove their shoes and walk around barefooted. At some point you can ask that they close their eyes and listen to the different sounds around them — even better if they cover their eyes with a bandana or eye mask. If there are edible plants nearby, perhaps they could lick or taste the leaves. Clearly, this will be at their own risk but it's a good idea for you to be familiar with plants that should not be interacted with, e.g. foxgloves and nettles. Dandelions, sorrel and mugwort are all good candidates for tasting. It's a good idea to have some bottled water for rinsing the plants before licking and obviously try and ensure that such plants are unlikely to be contaminated by dog or sheep excrement.

When participants have constructed their poems, ask that they write them out again neatly with white space between every line. The lines are now separated by folding and tearing so there's no need for scissors. The individual lines should then be pooled and each person blindly takes five lines and re-arranges them into a new poem.

PART TWO

How To Start a Writers' Group

INTRODUCTION

Starting a new writers' group is an adventure; an exciting journey into the unknown. And not only for you but also for those who will join you on this venture.

There are two things you will need at the outset — a passion for writing and a desire to help others on their writing journey. That's it. Provided you're committed, everything else will fall into place once you've made the decision.

Your job will be as facilitator; a role that ensures the meetings are productive and enjoyable. You'll soon find what works and what doesn't but there are guidelines in Appendix II that will help you on the way, including advice on how to deal with any potential problems that may arise. Please don't be put off by the mention of problems. Problems are rare within writing groups because everyone is there for the same reason. But in any group of people things can arise that need dealing with and, as facilitator, it will be your job to sort them out. It's best to be prepared for all eventualities.

CHAPTER 5
Preparing the Ground

STEP 1: Choose Your Venue

In my experience, most established writers' groups have between six and twelve members and this is the number you should aim for. Bear in mind though, that a group starting up from scratch will probably begin with less than six.

Your first job is to find a venue that is large enough to accommodate expected numbers. I recommend you start with your local library. I live in the North West of England and have found the library services very accommodating. Not only do they provide a room at no charge but most of the libraries also provide free tea and coffee. The upside of being in a library is that you are kept in the loop for literary events and will get help and free marketing should you progress to organising a writing group event. One of the groups I'm involved with independently published an anthology of poems and short stories which we entered into a competition arranged by NAWG (National Association of Writers' Groups). Our main central library helped us to organise a book launch in the library lecture theatre where we each read out excerpts from our contribution. The library sold tickets for the event on Eventbrite through their website. There was free wine and juice and each ticket holder got a complimentary copy of the anthology. The small profit at the end of the night helped towards the cost of members attending a conference later in the year. Libraries have the funding and the resources to help so why not use them?

They will even help you attract members when you first start up and are only too happy to pursue new avenues to promote their services.

If your local library is not so accommodating, or maybe doesn't have the space, you can often find a local pub or cafe happy to accommodate your group in a quiet corner. One of the groups I run meets twice a month; once in the local library and once in a local eatery. The only thing you have to be mindful of when choosing such a venue is background music, which can be very distracting. If it's a quiet time for trade a polite request for the music to be turned down is usually met with a good response.

I wouldn't recommend a venue where the room has to be paid for because that will necessitate you appointing a treasurer and charging people for attending. This may work for a stable group where attendance can always be relied on but, in my experience, writing groups attract a wide variety of people with varying commitment and proficiency and I think it's important that people do not feel under any financial obligation, especially in these difficult times. It's also quite important to keep the group relatively small. Any more than twelve and it's difficult to manage the time for feedback on individual work. Of course, if the room has to be paid for the charge per person will be much higher if numbers are low. However, if this is your only option then you will need to decide if members will be required to pay regardless of attendance. If members only pay on attendance, you could well find yourself out of pocket if fewer than expected turn up for any of the meetings. The alternative is to charge a monthly membership fee but this necessitates a huge organisational commitment. My philosophy is always to keep things as simple as possible. If things get complicated there is a tendency to feel over-whelmed. If that happens, the adventure may never get off the ground.

If all else fails you could take turns at meeting at each other's houses.

Room Set Up

Whichever venue you decide on, you must make sure that the room is large enough to accommodate at least ten people and, preferably, will house a table large enough for everyone to sit around. That way everyone can see everyone else and there is no hierarchy in the seating arrangement. It's important to build up trust within the group and this seating arrangement encourages that. It also means that if anyone is a little hard of hearing, lip reading can assist them. There should also be enough room for each person to have enough individual space for them to write comfortably or use a laptop.

STEP 2: Decide How Often You Will Meet

You need to decide when your group will meet. Will it be during the day or in the evening? During the week or at the weekend? This is your decision as the founder of the group, so pick a time that suits you — a time and day when you are as certain as you can be that you will always be available. Bear in mind that a group meeting during the day on a weekday will likely mainly attract retired people. If you want to attract younger people, then evenings or weekends may be better.

How often will you meet? Some groups meet weekly, some fortnightly, some monthly. It's entirely up to you to decide how much time you want to give to this venture. One of my groups initially met monthly but the meetings proved so useful that it wasn't long before we made the decision to meet more often. We now meet fortnightly.

STEP 3: Getting Members

What sort of people do you want in your group? Do you have any preferences? Do you want people who have never done any serious writing before or people who are already committed on the journey? Do you want poets? novelists? fiction writers? non-fiction writers? Or a good mixture of all of them? In my experience it's better to keep this remit as open as possible. The writing exercises in Part One are designed to stimulate creativity in every genre and every mode of writing and members will be surprised at what is produced when they are stretched beyond their comfort zones. Novelists can get experience writing snappy, descriptive sentences by writing poetry and poets can expand their creativity by writing short stories.

If you have chosen a library venue it is important that you do not exclude anyone who is interested in joining. Your library will have a policy on this, which you should ask to be informed of. The only stipulation I would make is that you need to decide at the outset whether you will accept the under eighteens into your group. Accepting minors puts you into a metaphorical minefield and I recommend that you stipulate from the outset that it is an adult group. Apart from the onerous responsibility and cost of having to get DBS checked (Disclosure and Barring Service), there will be problems if any of the writers wish to share work with adult content. One of the groups I'm involved with had this problem and it wasn't easy to sort things out. One of our members writes erotic fiction which neither she, nor any other members, would have been happy sharing with a minor. Despite this, the mother of a fourteen year old was insistent that she was prepared to take responsibility for whatever her daughter was exposed to. Unfortunately, the law is not so accommodating. We had, therefore, to decline admission though we did direct her to a more appropriate group through the library children's service.

STEP 4: Advertising

You won't need to pay for this and there's very little to do in the way of promotion. If you've chosen a library as the venue, the library staff will do a lot of the marketing for you at no cost, often in the form of flyers distributed around the borough and also through email distribution lists and monthly newsletter or something similar.

Free local papers are a wonderful platform and editors are always on the lookout for local stories. Usually you will be interviewed on the telephone and asked for a photograph. Alternatively, most editors will be only too happy for you to draft a brief article about yourself explaining why you're setting up the group and what you hope to achieve.

Make use too of any community notice boards. It's not difficult to produce a simple A5 flyer at home. These can be pinned on notice boards in local supermarkets or in libraries. If you have a Facebook page, make use of it. And of course, there are Twitter and Instagram. If you're not computer savvy, or are disinclined to use these social platforms, it's really not a problem. You'll do very well without them.

Make it clear on all the promotional material where and how often the group will meet, and the time and duration of the meetings. Also include your contact details (mobile or email) for anyone who requires more information.

CHAPTER 6
Running the Group

The First Meeting

You'll no doubt be nervous and full of trepidation wondering who's going to turn up and indeed whether anyone will turn up. Arrive at least fifteen minutes before the start and sit quietly composing yourself. Whatever happens, everything will be fine and I can (almost) guarantee you will not be left sitting alone. Why not spend the waiting time working on your current project?

Meet And Greet

As people drift in, as they will, make them feel welcome while explaining there will be proper introductions when everyone has arrived. It's an excellent idea to suggest that people help themselves to tea or coffee on arrival if it's available. In a pub or cafe suggest that everyone purchases a drink before sitting down.

There follows a brief agenda for the first meeting but obviously this is flexible, so don't get stressed if things don't go to plan. The most important thing is that participants enjoy themselves and feel it was time well spent. You can open the meeting however you like but my advice is to make it as informal as possible.

If the meeting was advertised as starting at 2pm, start at 2pm. There's nothing worse for those who have made the effort to get there on time than to have to wait for stragglers.

1. Introduce yourself and explain why you've started the group. Give a **very brief** account of your writing experience/accomplishments to date.

2. Ask everyone, in turn, to introduce themselves in the same way. Make it clear that the focus should be on their writing ambitions/accomplishments and not on their personal lives or situations. There will be time for more personal exchanges once the group is up and running and relationships start to form.

3. Ask those present what they would like to get out of the meetings. What's important to them? Have they any ideas about what format should be followed? Give your own views and suggestions. A format that works well is for a two hour meeting where the first hour is spent on one of the writing exercises from Part One and the second hour spent on giving feedback on individual work-in-progress. As the founder of the group, I suggest you present this format as a *fait accompli*, at least until the group is up and running.

If feedback is to be part of the meetings it is essential that members are clear about word limits and are advised to bring along hard copy print-outs of the piece requiring feedback. Those without access to a home printer can be advised to use library facilities, though libraries do charge for that.

4. Agree a format and make sure everyone is happy with it.

5. Pass round a piece of paper and ask everyone to write down their contact details. Emails are usually sufficient but you may like to ask for telephone numbers as well. Make sure everyone is happy to be included on the group's email

distribution list. Explain that this will mainly be used, especially initially, simply to remind people of the date of the next meeting.

6. Include time for questions or just general chatting.

7. Close the meeting on time. Thank everyone for coming and give the date of the next meet. If people want to stay behind, chatting, that's great. Be prepared for that to happen. Be sure to ask if they've enjoyed the session before closing. It will be easy to pick out those who haven't found the meeting useful.

If there is anyone who appears unhappy, perhaps speak to the person privately before leaving. 'I couldn't help noticing . . . is there anything I can do? Perhaps something I could do differently? We could discuss (whatever it is) at the next meeting.' If the response is that the group is not what was expected but yet it is clear that there was consensus amongst everyone else, then it is best to let the person go. Be sure to say 'thank you for coming and you are welcome to come back at any time.'

8. Go home and congratulate yourself on setting up a writers' group. And relax. Once the group has been formed it will evolve and mature under its own steam.

The Second Meeting

Managing groups of people can sometimes be rather like herding cats. I'm sure you've all heard that expression. It may be a cliché but it is nevertheless very true. It's important, therefore, to have a set agenda and make sure everyone follows it otherwise little will be accomplished and participants may start to feel it is not time well spent. To this end, it's a good idea to produce a handout for the second meeting detailing what was agreed in the first meeting. It should include the time plan and word limits of work to be shared for feedback.

I produce a handout for my group that details the format of the meetings and the word count limit for any work-in-progress requiring feedback. It also contains a reminder that printouts of written work are required. You'll find a copy of my handout in Appendix I. Please feel free to use it or modify it as necessary. As well as giving it out at the second meeting, I suggest you also give a copy to any new members that join once the group is up and running.

Flexibility is important where time allows but adherence to the agreed format is essential for larger groups to ensure that everyone gets a fair hearing. A handout is useful for bringing the group back on task and reminding them of the time constraints.

Routine Maintenance

It's a good idea to send an email the day before every meeting, just to remind participants of the date and time. Encourage members to email apologies for absences if unable to attend. This is more important when the group is quite small and also during the holiday season. It just means that you can organise the time more easily knowing that those absent at the start won't be turning up late. It also fosters commitment and responsibility within the group.

You may find that you regularly need to remind participants that if feedback is sought on a work-in-progress then the word limit must be adhered to. As mentioned earlier, it's also a good idea to insist on members providing hard copies of any scripts requiring feedback. It's well nigh impossible to give good constructive feedback just by listening to a piece being read out loud. It, therefore, goes without saying that everyone must come to the meeting armed with at least one pen.

Some writing groups opt to set up a website. While this can be useful in attracting new members and for showcasing the work being produced, it does not come without a cost — both financial and time. If the group does decide to go down this route, it's essential that someone is appointed web master and the website is kept fresh and up to date.

CHAPTER 7
Giving and Receiving Feedback

In my opinion, getting feedback from other writers is the most important function of a writers' group. It is invaluable and essential if one's writing is to improve and develop.

In one of my writing groups, I did initially set up a rota for feedback to try and ensure each piece received a thirty minute slot for in-depth feedback. However, this became onerous due to sickness and holidays making it necessary to juggle and swap slots for absences. These days I ask at the start of the meetings who has work requiring feedback. The time available is then split equally amongst them. As facilitator it's up to you to clock watch and carry out strict time management so that everyone gets their full allotted time.

It does no harm to remind people at the outset that the time they have been allocated is for reading the work out loud and receiving feedback. It is not time for them to defend their work or give lengthy explanations of why they wrote what they did. Feedback sprinkles written work with gold dust so participants should make sure they make the most of the time they've been allocated.

Giving Feedback

There are two ways to read a script — as a writer and as a reader. As a member of a writing group, it is helpful to try and wear both hats at the same time while giving a little more weight to your experience as a reader. Try and frame your feedback from the experience you had reading the piece. Were the characters believable? Were you transported into the setting? Always keep in mind that you are not the author. Your aim is to help the author achieve what he or she is trying to accomplish with the piece. You may not agree with the direction taken or the style in which it is written, but all that is irrelevant. All that matters is that the writer gets across to the reader what was intended.

Feedback can be written or oral. The latter is soon forgotten which is why I strongly recommend giving written feedback on hard copies of the work. This is of far more use to the writer as it can be taken home, allowing time to carefully consider the feedback and make changes if necessary.

When offering feedback, it's a good idea to first find something positive to say about the piece before launching into what you think doesn't work. Doing this will make the receiver more receptive to what is to follow. If you genuinely cannot find anything to praise, perhaps say that the piece shows a lot of promise. However, in my experience, there is always something to praise, something that works well.

The most important thing is to be specific and honest. If you think, for instance, that the pace is too slow or maybe there's too much exposition, refer to a specific part of the script that illustrates this. Similarly, if you really liked a particular turn of phrase or the development of an idea, point this out with examples.

I personally lap up brutal feedback. It's the best way to learn and improve quickly, but others may be destroyed by feedback that is too negative. Feedback should, therefore, be tailored, if possible, to the personality of the recipient. However, feedback that does nothing more than praise the work is no good to anyone and trying to be overly diplomatic may not get the point across.

Problems with sentence structure, syntax, grammar, punctuation and spelling are also important to flag up if it leads to ambiguities or distractions within the writing. There may also be stylistic problems that the reader may find irritating. For instance, over-use of a particular word. Critical feedback on these things, however, must be tempered with the fact that writers have different styles and just because one writer's voice does not resonate with someone else does not necessarily mean it is wrong. It's up to the writer to decide what to take on board and what to disregard. It's also important to bear in mind that grammar, like writing style, is at the mercy of fashion trends. You only have to read text speak or even some of the literary acclaimed novels of today to see this is true. One novel I read a couple of years ago, used no punctuation at all. Despite being a difficult read, it won many literary prizes.

Giving feedback is an art form and you will find lots of information and advice on the web should you wish to improve proficiency in this skill. As a member of a writing group all you really need to remember is that you should strive to give feedback that is constructive, helpful, honest and kind. If you keep this in mind, you won't go far wrong.

Remember, dishonest or flowery non-specific praise, just to be kind, helps no one.

Strictly speaking, suggestions as to how the piece could be improved should really only be given if requested. However, members should not be overly concerned about breaching rules of guidance if doing that inhibits what they wish to express about another's work if they believe it will be helpful.

Finally, it is important to remember that the feedback you give is your opinion of another's work. It is not necessarily right or true and you should never be affronted if your advice is rejected. The writer ALWAYS has the final word on his or her own work and that should be respected.

Receiving Feedback

"Remember: when people tell you something's wrong or doesn't work for them, they are almost always right. When they tell you exactly what they think is wrong and how to fix it, they are almost always wrong."   Neil Gaiman

Writing style is a very personal business and every writer must strive to find his or her own 'voice'. Sometimes, the person giving the feedback may suggest other ways of expressing an idea. It's up to you, as the recipient of the feedback, to separate the wheat from the chaff, keeping what you believe enhances the work, and disregarding what doesn't. The final decision is always yours and you must never feel bad about disagreeing with feedback you've been given. No matter how carefully phrased, feedback is often subjective. No one is infallible. But if you choose not to take it on board, be sure you know why you disagree. It may be that your story needs a little tweaking, just to avoid other readers having the same concern. Be aware that feedback may point out elements of your writing that you had been feeling good about. If this happens, be sure to look for a kernel of truth in what was said. Remember, all suggestions are given in good faith, to help you on your writing journey.

Whether or not you agree with what was said, it's only polite to make a point of thanking the person giving the feedback. A defensive response, justifying why you wrote what you did, will do nothing but dissuade members from giving feedback again. Remember, your goal is to improve your story.

If feedback prompts disagreements about any particular point, it's up to the facilitator to gently point out that time is at a premium and perhaps the discussion could be continued privately after the meeting is finished. Generally, I think it's a good idea to ask at the outset that feedback is not responded to.

We listen to feedback, we do not argue with it.

CONCLUSION

This book has evolved since its inception, as all books do, and grown during the period of its writing. I started out with only fifty exercises but life continued on its chaotic trajectory, presenting me with more and more ideas every day. The same can happen to you if you are receptive to the world around you. Life is bursting with potential and creative ideas for a writer, their number limited only by your imagination.

If you do not currently belong to a writers' group, I hope this book has tempted you to either join one or has encouraged you to start your own local group. Writers need a nurturing place to develop and fellow writers can be the fertilizer in your field of words. They can also be the source of great friendship and fun.

I'm confident that you will find the exercises in this book both productive and enjoyable. Digging deep into the creative genius that is part of human consciousness is more psychologically rewarding than anything else I can think of. We are co-creators of the world we live in after all.

Which brings me onto the subject of dreams — the night-time sort. I find a lot of inspiration for my writing in my dreams and I have written a number of books on the subject. For those of you who wish to know more about this, I recommend my book 'Creative Writing for Dreamers', (of course I do!) It takes a fresh approach to creativity by tapping directly into the source of the creative genius we all possess. It includes fifteen fun techniques to use on your dreams with five additional techniques to use during a dream drought.

I would like to leave you with a quote that a fellow writer sent me the other day. I have tried, unsuccessfully, to discover the author but it is too good a quote not to share.

Only a writer . . .

. . . can hold a conversation with people who don't exist.

. . . can wear pyjamas all day and lose all sense of reality.

. . . can have an internet search history that is more terrifying than that of a serial killer.

And a final warning.

Beware! Once you've been bitten by the writing bug, you will be a slave to the pen forever.

There is no cure.

APPENDIX I
FORMAT OF MEETINGS.

Sample handout showing session structure for a two hour meeting, twice monthly.

Agenda for FIRST MEETING of the month.
(Name of Venue, time and length of session)

The first hour of the session is devoted to a writing exercise and/or discussion of the craft of writing plus AOB.

The second hour will be devoted to giving feedback on private work, restricted to 500 words max. The time will be split amongst those requiring feedback.

Agenda for SECOND MEETING of the month.
(Name of Venue, time and length of session)

At these sessions, the full two hours will be devoted to giving feedback on private work. The time will be split equally amongst all who have brought work for feedback.

Feedback at these sessions is always honest so new members must be prepared to accept the feedback in the generous manner in which it is offered.

Work Presented For Feedback:

1. Word limit is generally 500 words for the first session and 1000 - 1300 for the second. The piece can be anything you like, prose or poetry, fiction or non-fiction. Each person will have a limited amount of time so bear in mind that the longer

pieces will leave less time for feedback. Poems generally initiate more discussion/feedback so it's probably best to just bring along one even though the word count is small.

2. Can be a complete work or an extract.

3. Several printed copies of the work requiring feedback should be brought to the session to enable those feeding back to make notes on the hard copy.

4. It's helpful to give an introduction to/explanation of the piece. A short synopsis / 'story so far' included at the beginning of the printed copy is a good idea.

5. The piece should not be a first draft as these always require improvement. To gain the most from feedback the piece needs to be something you have worked on and feel you've gone as far as you can with it. If there's a part that you particularly want feedback on, please say so, (e.g. the opening paragraph or a part that you think needs more work but you're not sure how to develop it). This is especially important for longer pieces as it means the feedback will be more focussed.

APPENDIX II
HINTS AND TIPS FOR FACILITATORS

Enthuse And Encourage

Open every meeting with a smile and show a genuine interest in how everyone's doing. The members of your writing group will undoubtedly become your friends and often your confidants. Nourishing and growing the relationships will pay dividends not only with your writing but in mostly every area of your life.

One Of The Team

A good facilitator manages the group while appearing to be just another member of it. However, you will be the captain of the ship, steering the proceedings and keeping things on course. Your job is to try and make sure that expectations are met and that everyone feels like a valued and equal member. If this is to be achieved, and conflict and misunderstandings avoided, it is essential to listen attentively and be prepared to change direction if necessary.

Be aware that in any group of people difficulties can arise from time to time. As the facilitator of the group, it will be your responsibility to deal with problems the moment you spot them.

There follows some examples of behaviours that can cause difficulties in a group and how best to deal with them.

Staying Silent, Not Joining In Discussions

Every so often, ask those not participating to comment on whatever is being discussed. More often than not it's because the person is shy or feels lacking in the skills or experience necessary to join in. This is especially the case in mixed groups where the more experienced writers can unwittingly intimidate those less knowledgeable.

If feedback is being given on someone's work, it's usually best to go round the table, inviting everyone to speak in turn. That way, no one is missed out.

Always Arriving Late

Arriving late to a writing group can be very disruptive, especially if the group is busy with a writing exercise or is reading out work for feedback. Obviously sometimes it cannot be avoided but if it's a regular occurrence a quiet word on the side will usually suffice. In my experience, lateness in writing groups is not usually a problem as writers tend to be enthusiastic and committed creatures.

Distracted By Phone Messages Or Calls

Sometimes members need to be reminded to keep their phone on silent, or better still (if there is no necessity to keep it on) switched off altogether.

Dominating The Discussion

This is probably the biggest challenge you will face as a facilitator. In any group there is often at least one who likes to talk incessantly and digress at every opportunity. The best way to deal with it is to politely point out the time constraint and that there are others waiting to speak. Often this problem goes hand-in-hand with the overly vocal person losing focus and straying from the task. Again, politely bring them back to the task in hand.

Do As I Do

As a writer one never stops learning. Fashions in style and grammar change. Different genres have different styles. Writers too have individual styles which may not be to the liking of everyone. In creative writing there are no rights and no wrongs and this is a maxim that the group should remember. Suggestions for improvement are great. On the other hand, telling writers how to write will only stifle creativity.

Dealing With Conflict

Managing conflict is always difficult but, if not addressed, the fallout can result in the break-up of the group. The only way to deal with it is to bring it out in the open and talk about it with the people involved. Find out what the problem is and encourage discussion and apologies on both sides. It's also a good idea to let both parties know how valuable they are to the group and how you don't want to lose either of them. This will usually result in an amicable settlement.

Sometimes though, where one party remains a disruptive element, it's up to you to request, as diplomatically as possible, that the person refrains from upsetting other members, otherwise you may have to ask them to leave the group.

RESOURCES

National Association of Writers and Groups (NAWG)
https://www.nawg.co.uk

More writing exercises

Reedsy. 100+ Creative Writing Exercises for Fiction Authors https://blog.reedsy.com/writing-exercises/

'The Writer's Toolbox' by Jamie Cat Callan. Creative games and exercises for inspiring the 'Write' side of your brain.

'What If? Writing Exercises for Fiction Writers' by Anne Bernays and Pamela Painter. Collins (2005)

Places where the (edited) results of your writing exercises can be showcased:

https://www.fridayflashfiction.com/

https://101words.org/submit-your-stories/

General

https://www.thesaurus.com/

The author's websites:
www.docdreamuk.com
www.joharthan.co.uk

Joan Harthan, PhD

Creative Writing for Dreamers

Release your Inner Daemon

ISBN: 9798730174535

Do you know that you can use your dreams to tap directly into the source of your creative genius? With a selection of novel exercises, this book will show you how to unlock your hidden potential.

~ 89 ~

Printed in Great Britain
by Amazon

80993117R00058